Shapes and Colors

Words by Nina Filipeck

Illustrated by Jan Smith

book-studio

Tim Smith
26 Main Street
Anytown
USA 11100

Tim gets a card.

What shape is the card?

What color is the envelope?

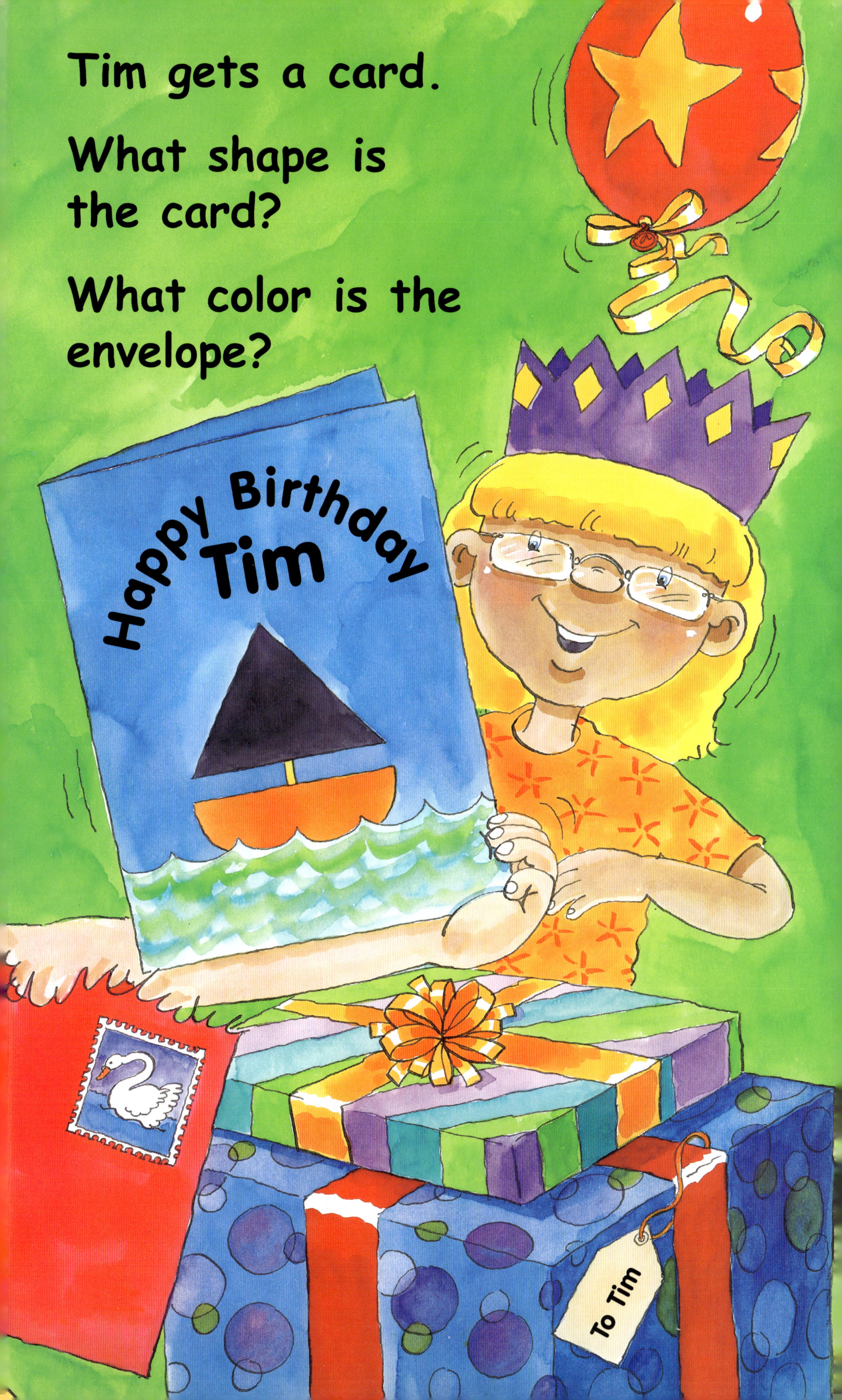

Tim gets a book.

What shape is the book?

What color is Tim's T-shirt?

Happy Birthday Tim

Dad gives Tim a big box.
Tim wonders what's inside.
What shape is the box?
What color is the ribbon?

It's a sailboat!

Tim carefully lifts it from the box.

What shape is the sail on the boat?

What color is the boat?

Mom gives out the drinks and lollipops.

What shape are the lollipops?

What color are the drinks?

Dad joins in the party games.

Tim gives Dad a party hat and a balloon.

What shape is the party hat?

What color is the balloon?

Everyone has a party favor bag and a piece of chocolate cake.

What shape can you see on the bag?

What color is the cake?

Tim makes a "thank you" card for Mom and Dad.

What shape is on the card?

What color is the table?